THIS BOOK BELONGS TO

_____

A Gardener's Journal

A FIVE-YEAR RECORD BOOK

CollinsPublishersSanFrancisco

A Division of HarperCollins*Publishers*

First published in USA 1995 by Collins Publishers San Francisco
Copyright © 1995 Collins Publishers San Francisco
Photographic copyright © Kathryn Kleinman
Styling: Michaele Thunen
Design: Kari Perin
Illustrations and Calligraphy: Lauren Allard
ISBN 0-00-649136-7
Printed in Singapore
1 3 5 7 9 10 8 6 4 2

Contents

January

The snow, the bitter cold,
Fell all the night;
And we awoke to see
The garden white.
And still the silvery flakes
Go whirling by,
White feathers fluttering
From a grey sky.
Beyond the gate, soft feet
In silence go,
Beyond the frosted pane
White shines the snow.

—F. Ann Elliott, "The Snow"

January

WEEK 1

Weather

Bulbs and Flowers

Shrubs and Trees

Lawns

Vegetables and Fruit

Greenhouse

Notes

Year

Year

Year

January

WEEK 2

	Year	Year

Weather

Bulbs and Flowers

Shrubs and Trees

Lawns

Vegetables and Fruit

Greenhouse

Notes

Year

Year

Year

January

WEEK 3

Weather

Bulbs and Flowers

Shrubs and Trees

Lawns

Vegetables and Fruit

Greenhouse

Notes

January

WEEK 4

Weather

Bulbs and Flowers

Shrubs and Trees

Lawns

Vegetables and Fruit

Greenhouse

Notes

Year

Year

Year

February

Still, in a way, nobody sees a flower;

really. It is so small. We haven't the

time and to see takes time, like to have

friends takes time. —Georgia O'Keeffe

February

WEEK 1

Weather

Bulbs and Flowers

Shrubs and Trees

Lawns

Vegetables and Fruit

Greenhouse

Notes

Year

Year

Year

February

WEEK 2

Weather

Bulbs and Flowers

Shrubs and Trees

Lawns

Vegetables and Fruit

Greenhouse

Notes

Year

Year

Year

February

WEEK 3

Weather

Bulbs and Flowers

Shrubs and Trees

Lawns

Vegetables and Fruit

Greenhouse

Notes

Year

Year

Year

February

WEEK 4

Year

Year

Weather

Bulbs and Flowers

Shrubs and Trees

Lawns

Vegetables and Fruit

Greenhouse

Notes

| *Year* | *Year* | *Year* |

March

"Yes, they are tiny growing things and they might be crocuses or snowdrops or daffodils," she whispered. She bent very close to them and sniffed the fresh scent of the damp earth. —Frances Hodgson Burnett, The Secret Garden

27

March

WEEK 1

Year	Year

Weather

Bulbs and Flowers

Shrubs and Trees

Lawns

Vegetables and Fruit

Greenhouse

Notes

Year	Year	Year

March

WEEK 2

Weather

Bulbs and Flowers

Shrubs and Trees

Lawns

Vegetables and Fruit

Greenhouse

Notes

Year

Year

Year

March

WEEK 3

Weather

_____

Bulbs and Flowers

_____

Shrubs and Trees

_____

Lawns

_____

Vegetables and Fruit

_____

Greenhouse

_____

Notes

_____

Year

Year

Year

March

WEEK 4

Weather

Bulbs and Flowers

Shrubs and Trees

Lawns

Vegetables and Fruit

Greenhouse

Notes

Year	Year	Year

35

April

Live in each season as it passes;
breathe the air, drink the drink,
taste the fruit, and resign yourself
to the influences of each.

—Henry David Thoreau

April

WEEK 1

Year	Year

Weather

Bulbs and Flowers

Shrubs and Trees

Lawns

Vegetables and Fruit

Greenhouse

Notes

April

WEEK 2

Weather

Bulbs and Flowers

Shrubs and Trees

Lawns

Vegetables and Fruit

Greenhouse

Notes

Year

Year

April

WEEK 3

Weather

Bulbs and Flowers

Shrubs and Trees

Lawns

Vegetables and Fruit

Greenhouse

Notes

Year

Year

Year

April

WEEK 4

Year	Year

Weather

Bulbs and Flowers

Shrubs and Trees

Lawns

Vegetables and Fruit

Greenhouse

Notes

Year

Year

Year

May

Flowers leave some of their
fragrance in the hand that
bestows them.
—Chinese proverb

May

WEEK 1

Year

Year

Weather

Bulbs and Flowers

Shrubs and Trees

Lawns

Vegetables and Fruit

Greenhouse

Notes

Year

Year

Year

49

May

WEEK 2

Year

Year

Weather

Bulbs and Flowers

Shrubs and Trees

Lawns

Vegetables and Fruit

Greenhouse

Notes

Year

_____

Year

_____

Year

_____

51

May

WEEK 3

Weather

Bulbs and Flowers

Shrubs and Trees

Lawns

Vegetables and Fruit

Greenhouse

Notes

Year

_____

Year

_____

Year

_____

53

May

WEEK 4

Weather

Bulbs and Flowers

Shrubs and Trees

Lawns

Vegetables and Fruit

Greenhouse

Notes

June

I was walking alone in my garden; there was great stillness among the branches and flowers, and more than common sweetness in the air; I heard a low and pleasant sound, and I knew not whence it came. At last I saw the broad leaf of a flower move, and underneath I saw a green procession of creatures, of the size and colour of green and grey grasshoppers, bearing a body laid out on a rose-leaf, which they buried with songs, and then disappeared. It was a fairy funeral.

—William Blake

June

WEEK 1

	Year	Year
Weather		
Bulbs and Flowers		
Shrubs and Trees		
Lawns		
Vegetables and Fruit		
Greenhouse		
Notes		

Year

Year

Year

June

WEEK 2

Weather

Bulbs and Flowers

Shrubs and Trees

Lawns

Vegetables and Fruit

Greenhouse

Notes

Year

Year

Year

June

WEEK 3

Year	Year

Weather

Bulbs and Flowers

Shrubs and Trees

Lawns

Vegetables and Fruit

Greenhouse

Notes

Year

Year

Year

June

WEEK 4

Weather

Bulbs and Flowers

Shrubs and Trees

Lawns

Vegetables and Fruit

Greenhouse

Notes

Year

_____

Year

_____

Year

_____

July

Working in the garden...gives me a profound feeling of inner peace. Nothing here is in a hurry. There is no rush toward accomplishment, no blowing of trumpets. Here is the great mystery of life and growth. Everything is changing, growing, aiming at something, but silently, unboastfully, taking its time. —Ruth Stout

67

July

WEEK 1

Weather

Bulbs and Flowers

Shrubs and Trees

Lawns

Vegetables and Fruit

Greenhouse

Notes

July

WEEK 2

Weather

Bulbs and Flowers

Shrubs and Trees

Lawns

Vegetables and Fruit

Greenhouse

Notes

Year

Year

Year

July

WEEK 3

Year

Year

Weather

Bulbs and Flowers

Shrubs and Trees

Lawns

Vegetables and Fruit

Greenhouse

Notes

Year

Year

Year

July

WEEK 4

Weather

Bulbs and Flowers

Shrubs and Trees

Lawns

Vegetables and Fruit

Greenhouse

Notes

August

As my Garden invites into it all the
Birds of the Country,... I value my
garden more for it being full of
Blackbirds than Cherries, and very
frankly give them Fruit for their
Songs. ——Joseph Addison

77

August

WEEK 1

	Year	Year
Weather		
Bulbs and Flowers		
Shrubs and Trees		
Lawns		
Vegetables and Fruit		
Greenhouse		
Notes		

Year	*Year*	*Year*

August

WEEK 2

Weather

Bulbs and Flowers

Shrubs and Trees

Lawns

Vegetables and Fruit

Greenhouse

Notes

Year

Year

Year

August

WEEK 3

Year

Year

Weather

Bulbs and Flowers

Shrubs and Trees

Lawns

Vegetables and Fruit

Greenhouse

Notes

Year	Year	Year

August

WEEK 4

Weather

Bulbs and Flowers

Shrubs and Trees

Lawns

Vegetables and Fruit

Greenhouse

Notes

September

It is the simple things of life that make living worthwhile, the sweet fundamental things such as love and duty, work and rest and living close to nature. —Laura Ingalls Wilder

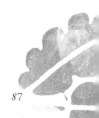

September

WEEK 1

Weather

Bulbs and Flowers

Shrubs and Trees

Lawns

Vegetables and Fruit

Greenhouse

Notes

Year

Year

Year

September

WEEK 2

Weather

Bulbs and Flowers

Shrubs and Trees

Lawns

Vegetables and Fruit

Greenhouse

Notes

Year

Year

Year

September

WEEK 3

Weather

Bulbs and Flowers

Shrubs and Trees

Lawns

Vegetables and Fruit

Greenhouse

Notes

September

WEEK 4

Year   Year

Weather

Bulbs and Flowers

Shrubs and Trees

Lawns

Vegetables and Fruit

Greenhouse

Notes

94

October

Even if something is left undone,

everyone must take time to sit

still and watch the leaves turn.

—Elizabeth Lawerence

October

WEEK 1

Weather

Bulbs and Flowers

Shrubs and Trees

Lawns

Vegetables and Fruit

Greenhouse

Notes

Year	*Year*	*Year*

October

	Year	Year

Weather

Bulbs and Flowers

Shrubs and Trees

Lawns

Vegetables and Fruit

Greenhouse

Notes

Year

Year

Year

October

WEEK 3

Weather

Bulbs and Flowers

Shrubs and Trees

Lawns

Vegetables and Fruit

Greenhouse

Notes

Year

Year

Year

October

WEEK 4

Year

Year

Weather

Bulbs and Flowers

Shrubs and Trees

Lawns

Vegetables and Fruit

Greenhouse

Notes

Year

Year

Year

November

I prefer winter and fall, when you feel

the bone structure in the landscape—

the loneliness of it—the dead feeling

of winter. Something waits beneath

it—the whole story doesn't show.

—Andrew Wyeth

107

November

WEEK 1

Weather

Bulbs and Flowers

Shrubs and Trees

Lawns

Vegetables and Fruit

Greenhouse

Notes

Year

Year

Year

November

WEEK 2

Weather

Bulbs and Flowers

Shrubs and Trees

Lawns

Vegetables and Fruit

Greenhouse

Notes

Year

Year

Year

November

WEEK 3

Weather

Bulbs and Flowers

Shrubs and Trees

Lawns

Vegetables and Fruit

Greenhouse

Notes

Year		Year		Year

November

WEEK 4

Weather

Bulbs and Flowers

Shrubs and Trees

Lawns

Vegetables and Fruit

Greenhouse

Notes

Year

Year

Year

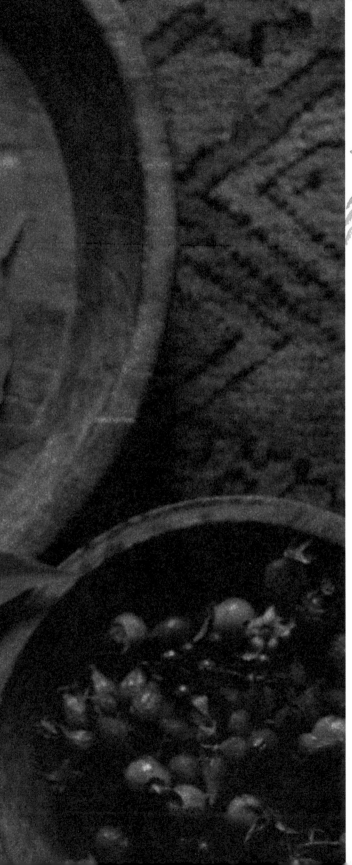

December

Nothing that is can pause or stay;

The moon will wax, the moon will

wane, The mist and cloud will turn

to rain, The rain to mist and cloud

again, Tomorrow be today.

—Henry Wadsworth Longfellow

December

WEEK 1

Year

Year

Weather

Bulbs and Flowers

Shrubs and Trees

Lawns

Vegetables and Fruit

Greenhouse

Notes

December

WEEK 2

Year

Year

Weather

Bulbs and Flowers

Shrubs and Trees

Lawns

Vegetables and Fruit

Greenhouse

Notes

Year

Year

Year

December

WEEK 3

Weather

Bulbs and Flowers

Shrubs and Trees

Lawns

Vegetables and Fruit

Greenhouse

Notes

Year

Year

Year

December

WEEK 4

Weather

Bulbs and Flowers

Shrubs and Trees

Lawns

Vegetables and Fruit

Greenhouse

Notes

Summary of Year One

	SPRING	SUMMER
Weather		
Bulbs and Flowers		
Shrubs and Trees		
Lawns		
Vegetables and Fruit		
Greenhouse		
Notes		

FALL

WINTER

Summary of Year Two

	SPRING	SUMMER
Weather		
Bulbs and Flowers		
Shrubs and Trees		
Lawns		
Vegetables and Fruit		
Greenhouse		
Notes		

FALL

WINTER

Summary of Year Three

	SPRING	SUMMER
Weather		
Bulbs and Flowers		
Shrubs and Trees		
Lawns		
Vegetables and Fruit		
Greenhouse		
Notes		

FALL

WINTER

Summary of Year Four

	SPRING	SUMMER
Weather		
Bulbs and Flowers		
Shrubs and Trees		
Lawns		
Vegetables and Fruit		
Greenhouse		
Notes		

FALL

_____
_____
_____
_____
_____
_____
_____
_____
_____
_____
_____
_____
_____
_____
_____
_____
_____
_____
_____
_____

WINTER

_____
_____
_____
_____
_____
_____
_____
_____
_____
_____
_____
_____
_____
_____
_____
_____
_____
_____

Summary of Year Five

	SPRING	SUMMER
Weather		
Bulbs and Flowers		
Shrubs and Trees		
Lawns		
Vegetables and Fruit		
Greenhouse		
Notes		

FALL   WINTER

Suppliers

Suppliers

Suppliers

Suppliers

Approximate Measures

LENGTH/WIDTH

- *A hand (closed) equals 4 inches*
- *A head (spread) equals 7-8 inches*
- *A foot equals 10-12 inches*
- *A pace (stride) equals 3 feet*

AREA

- *Acre equals 43,560 sq. feet*
- *Hectacre equals 2-1/2 acres*

LIQUID VOLUME

- *1 teaspoon equals 4 ml*
- *1 tablespoon equals 16 ml (1/2 fluid ounce)*
- *Household bucket equals 2 gallons (9 litres)*

MANURE/COMPOST

- *1 wheelbarrow load equals 10 pounds (enough for 10 sq. yards/90 sq. feet)*

TREES

- *Age: circumference of tree (inches) equals age of tree (years)*
- *Height equals distance of observer from tree when angle from observer's eye to tree top is approximately 45 degrees*